**LIBRARIES OI**

and why they ne

# LIBRARIES OF A LIFETIME

*and why they need to stay open*

## Chris Arnot

This edition published 2024 by:
Takahe Publishing Ltd.
Registered Office:
77 Earlsdon Street, Coventry CV5 6EL

Copyright © Chris Arnot 2024

ISBN 978-1-908837-31-8

The moral rights of the author have been asserted.

All rights reserved. This publication may not be reproduced, stored in a retrieval system or transmitted, in any form or by any means, electronic, mechanical, photocopying, recording or otherwise, without the prior permission of the publishers.

**TAKAHE PUBLISHING LTD. 2024**

*Dedicated to the many volunteers who give up so much of their time to keep so many libraries open against the odds – and particularly to those who do it for my "local".*

## Contents

| | | |
|---|---|---|
| – | Introduction | 1 |
| 1. | Where My Love of Books Began | 5 |
| 2. | Birmingham Central(s) | 13 |
| 3. | Whitechapel Library, Aldgate East | 25 |
| 4. | Westminster to Bloomsbury and Beyond | 35 |
| 5. | Two Budding Brains Given Life by Yorkshire Libraries | 51 |
| 6. | The Car that Crashed into the Crime Books | 63 |
| 7. | Nottingham Central(s) | 69 |
| 8. | From Locarno to Library | 79 |
| 9. | My Beloved "Local" | 95 |
| – | Postscript | 115 |

## *Introduction*

Shortly before finishing this book, I found another book on libraries that I've since found difficult to put down. It's called *The Last Library*, by Freya Sampson, and is what you might call a work of fiction very much based on fact.

The fact is that libraries all over the country, from remote villages to small towns, to bustling suburbs in big cities, are facing closure.

Why?

Because local authorities are facing financial problems, largely caused by continuous squeezing by central government. Since I started writing this book, Birmingham and Nottingham have both declared themselves bankrupt.

Some twenty five more libraries are thought to be under threat of closure in Birmingham, the city where I grew up and which features in the first two chapters.

In Nottingham, the city where I worked for much of the nineteen seventies, the bankruptcy declaration came shortly after the impressively spacious central library had just opened its doors [see chapter seven].

*Libraries of a Lifetime*

So are libraries a waste of precious public money at a time when factual information and works of fiction can be read on-line?

No, is the short answer to that. This book, I hope, provides a longer, more convincing argument. And this quote below, from Freya Sampson's all-too-relevant work of fiction, is a succinct summary of why local libraries still provide a vital service.

The words are put into the mouth of June Jones, a hitherto shy and somewhat timid library assistant still mourning the death of her mother who had been a much livelier and more loveable librarian. Nonetheless, when the local council is on the verge of voting for closure, June somehow stands up to be counted with the following inspiring intervention from the public gallery:

> *"... Libraries aren't just about books. They're places where an eight-year-old boy can have his eyes opened up to the wonders of the world, and where a lonely eighty-year-old woman can come for some vital human contact. Where a teenager can find a precious quiet space to do her homework and a recently arrived immigrant can find a new community. Libraries are places where everyone, rich or poor, wherever they come from in the world, can feel safe. Where they can access information that will empower them."*

*Introduction*

Amen to that. And thanks to those who now volunteer to keep open so many of those havens of "human contact", information and inspiration. My current "local" is a classic example, as you can read in the final chapter.

For now, though, let's begin at the beginning . . .

## Libraries of a Lifetime

*Chapter One*

## ***Where My Love of Books Began***

"To begin at the beginning . . . "

Yes, that's the opening line of *Under Milk Wood*. And no, there's not much comparison between Northfield in south Birmingham and Llareggub, somewhere in fictional rural Wales, the setting around which Dylan Thomas spun his mesmeric words. "Bugger all," you might say.

That's what Thomas said when asked to explain where he came up with the name of the fictional village that he immortalised. Try spelling Llareggub backwards and you'll see what he meant.

And Northfield?

Well, to quote opening line from another poet, "I remember, I remember" * growing up there and being taken by my parents to my very first library in the distant days of the 1950s.

By the mid-1960s I'd become a long-term regular, usually calling in on Saturday mornings. The afternoons were for playing football or cricket in the adjoining park with mates who were derisory about my growing love of words. Undaunted, I carried on browsing and borrowing.

*My first library looking little changed, externally at least*

Picked up a copy of *Under Milk Wood* there, having heard Richard Burton's unforgettable rendering of those sublime lines. But I tended to veer towards the works of novelists dubbed "angry young men". They'd come from working-class backgrounds in towns and cities well to the north of London and their works had been made into gritty, grey films – the equivalent of "kitchen-sink" dramas.

## 1 - *Where My Love of Books Began*

Northfield's suitably twin-setted and pearled librarians of the day made their disapproval all too evident through furrowed frowns and clicking tongues when I arrived back at their desk with works by the likes of Alan Sillitoe, Stan Barstow and John Braine. Apart from anything else, they contained what the BBC would dub "scenes of a sexual nature".

Times change. So do attitudes.

What hadn't changed almost sixty years on, when I'd finally completed my long hike from Northfield Station, was the frontage of Northfield Library. It was still solidly cemented red brick with sash windows either side of a decorative doorway and above a handsome plaque outlining the building's history.

The library had been built – or rather rebuilt – in 1914. Not because of a stray German Zeppelin, I might add. The outbreak of the First World War was still some months away when the original building had been burnt down, apparently by the local suffragettes.

It had first been erected in 1906, maybe in more flamboyantly Edwardian style. Like many another local library, the money had been donated by the Scottish-American philanthropist Andrew Carnegie. And, like many another building in south Birmingham, the land had been provided by the Cadbury family from nearby Bourneville.

*Libraries of a Lifetime*

*A short history of a building a hundred and ten years old*

You won't be surprised to hear that the library's interior had changed somewhat since my day. A glance to the right once I'd stepped through the doors confirmed that.

The "newspaper room" had gone. Once stuffed with "broadsheets" and magazines, it had been the place where I found my first job. In journalism, that is. I'd spent the

## 1 - Where My Love of Books Began

summer of 1970 working at the chocolate factory run by the aforesaid Cadbury family to pay off my debts after three years away at university.

No, they were nothing like the debts that graduates are lumbered with today. In fact, I'd just about seen them off by the time I edged my way into that sparsely populated part of the library where one newspaper peruser was already snoring loudly over a crumpled copy of *The Times*.

By that time I'd become a regular reader of *The Guardian*, a paper that I would write for many year later. For now though I had my eyes on the *Daily Telegraph*, an organ of Conservative values that I wouldn't have been seen dead with on the streets outside.

The "Torygraph", as we long-haired "lefties" called it, nonetheless harboured advertisements for the few jobs available at the time on newspapers and magazines.

The only one that I could find on that fateful day in the reading room was on *Men's Wear Magazine*. In Soho Square, W1, if you please. And before you ask, no it wasn't *that* kind of magazine, just a respectable trade paper for those involved in the menswear business.

At least they took a chance and offered me the job, including a morning of training in journalism every week at the London College of Printing.

*Libraries of a Lifetime*

Pat Freestone, an old pal from student days, had a flat in the East End and offered me the chance to "kip" on the floor there while I looked around for a place of my own.

Pat's flat was on the Mile End Road, not far from Whitechapel Library, Aldgate East, which had been immortalised in an evocative poem by Bernard Kops on how the books in there had transformed his life.

We may well be going back to that "orchard within for the heart and the mind" in a later chapter, but for now let's get back to Northfield Library, Birmingham South.

You won't be surprised to hear that there are now computer screens everywhere, including the space where the old newspaper room once stood apart. Not forgetting an upstairs section that didn't exist "back in my day".
The librarians, however, remained to the left of the downstairs section, clearly visible as you entered. Changed a bit, mind you, since the proverbial "twin set and pearls" days.

I just happened to fall into conversation with one of them whose bare shoulders were covered in tattoos.

No matter. Bernie Keeley-Noone was friendly and welcoming. She'd worked in the library service for over thirty five years, it seemed. "Touch wood, we're still open full-time at this one," she confirmed – a reference to the ongoing threats to library services from squeezed local government spending.

## 1 - Where My Love of Books Began

As she spoke, another pre-school child came in with his mum and headed excitedly towards the already well-populated children's section. The school holidays were fast approaching and plans were already in place for the "reading challenge", Bernie assured me.

"The aim is to get those who take part in it to read six books in six weeks," she explained. "We advertise it in local schools beforehand and the kids seem to love it. Those who manage it are given a medal and some gifts, like pencils or fridge magnets."

Makes sense at a time when the lure of computer games is all too evident. What the librarians of my childhood and youth would have made of it, mind you, heaven only knows.

Having said goodbye to Bernie, I strolled down between the shelves and noticed that one was labelled "Large Print". Somewhat more politically correct, perhaps, than what it used to be many decades ago: "For the Nearly Blind".

Nearby were biographies on everyone from TS Elliot to Roy Hudd and works from novelists as diverse as Don de Lillo and Jeffrey Archer.

Suddenly it felt good to be back at the beginning. And by that I mean where it began for me. Not only was the library of my childhood and youth still open; it seemed to

*Libraries of a Lifetime*

be thriving, even on a midweek morning. Bigger and much lighter too.

At the far end were wide windows looking out over Victoria Common, as Northfield Park is still labelled to this day. Time, perhaps, to take a stroll across the expansive spread of city greenery where I went on my first swing, kicked my first football and finally connected with my first cricket ball.

Beyond, at the very top end, was the busy Bristol Road offering a route into the city centre some five miles away. It was time to "ger on the buz", as town-bound Brummies tended to say, and seek out the latest version of the central library.

* *"I Remember, I Remember" is the title and opening line of a poem by Thomas Hood, written in 1826. It's also the title of Philip Larkin's poem about Coventry, the city where he grew up.*

*Chapter Two*

## *Birmingham Central(s)*

Everything had "changed, changed utterly", to quote WB Yeats in a very different context. I'd like to add that "a terrible beauty is born". Instead let's just say that Birmingham is always changing, and sometimes changing utterly – as in the 1960s and '70s when ornate Victorian and Edwardian structures were being bulldozed away and replaced by concrete and glass blocks. Nearby new ring roads and flyovers were rising above the rubble to accommodate the cars that had been designed and assembled at local factories.

There have been three libraries here in the city centre in my lifetime. And, to my eyes at least, the latest one is better looking than the "brutalist" building in so-called Paradise Circus. That, in its turn, had replaced the Victorian haven of leather-bound tomes that I remember from days in the late 1960s when I'd come home from university and spend part of my "vacations" researching in the sepulchral silence imposed by the librarians of the day.

Prince Charles (as he was at the time) maintained in a television documentary that what was then still referred to as "the new library" resembled "a place where books are incinerated, not kept".

Well, it had been slotted together in concrete and glass and opened in 1974. The Prince's proclamation was broadcast in 1988, by which time the concrete panelling had been badly stained by rain and heaven knows what else.

Nonetheless, there was quite a kerfuffle when the proposed closure was announced. The Twentieth Century Society was particularly voluble in its opposition to the demolition of a library that the World Monuments Fund had placed on its list of "significant buildings at risk" in 2011.

Books and much else were moved some hundred and fifty metres away to the latest "new" Library of Birmingham in Centenary Square in the summer of 2013. And the building that had housed them was finally demolished three years later, despite two attempts by English Heritage to have it listed.

By then Birmingham had already "changed, changed utterly" heaven knows how many times. The car industry was in deathly decline – even the one-time Austin factory in Longbridge had closed eight years previously – and the emphasis now was on attracting visitors, including concert and conference-goers, to the city centre.

Hence the International Conference Centre, housing the much-praised acoustics of the concert hall and leading to a canal basin that had been transformed from a filthy cesspit into a visitor attraction lined with restaurants and bars.

## 2 - Birmingham Central(s)

The ICC fronts on to Centenary Square that also houses the "new" repertory theatre, opened a mere forty two years before the library that adjoins it.

* * *

Tom Epps, the library's senior services manager, strolled out just before the doors closed at six pm on a pleasant Thursday evening and we strolled on towards the site of the previous library. Oh yes, and the one before that.

On the way he told me how he'd come to Birmingham from his parents' home in Hampshire back in the mid-1980s to study economics at university. After dabbling in accountancy as a post-grad, he took what was supposed to be a temporary job in the business library. "Twenty five years on and I'm still here."

Albeit in a more important job in a different building, I pointed out before going on to ask about his view of the difference between the current library and its predecessor.

"The 1970s building had been designed to meet the public's expectations of what a library should be at the time," he replied. "So there was an assumption that people would come to read or study quietly and an emphasis on security."

It's worth remembering at this point that the so-called brutalist building, designed by John Madin, had opened in 1974. That was the year the IRA had planted bombs in two Birmingham pubs, killing twenty one people and injuring many more.

*Libraries of a Lifetime*

So it's not surprising, perhaps, that Tom remembered "an emphasis on book security" before going on to remind me that "at one point you couldn't go upstairs with a bag. You'd have to leave it downstairs."

He also recalled "an assumption that people would come to read or study quietly" before acknowledging that "librarians could be quite fearsome in those days."

As I well remember.

My memories of the library before the library before last are somewhat vague. Perhaps that was because, as I mentioned earlier, I only called in during vacations in my student days. And those visits had to be fitted in with whatever "holiday job" that I'd taken on, whether it was cutting grass with a scythe in a cemetery or being a sandwich-board man advertising an art shop in one of the city's more upmarket arcades.

Although the Victorian library had long gone by the time Tom arrived in Brum, he was happy to remind me of its location.

Ah yes, right next door to the pillared portals of the town hall. And the School of Music, now part of Birmingham City University, was right next door to the old library.

The remains of both are now buried under yet another Birmingham building site. This one's called Paradise, believe it or not.

## 2 - Birmingham Central(s)

"There used to be a sign for 'Paradise Place' round the back of the Madin Library," Tom recalled. "By the late nineties the visual irony was stark. Damp concrete, poor graffiti, pigeon detritus, litter and general skankiness prevailed. However, the name 'Paradise' has been used for this part of town for a long time. I think Paradise Street existed in the late eighteenth century."

Paradise is also now the name of the passageway lined with restaurants and offices linking Centenary Square with Chamberlain Square.

*Monument to Joseph Chamberlain overlooking the town hall with site of the first central library to the right*

*Libraries of a Lifetime*

\* \* \*

You may not be surprised to learn that the square is named after Joseph Chamberlain, a major figure in Birmingham's history. No relation, however, to the architect John Chamberlain who was called upon to redesign the "old" library when it was gutted by fire in 1879.

His Venetian-Gothic style received mixed reviews, apparently, but his Shakespeare Room received much praise for its Elizabethan style. Bedecked with carvings and ornate metalwork, I vaguely recall gazing at it with awe in my student days. Well, I was studying English literature at the time.

Tom reminded me that the first folio of the Bard's complete works was published in 1623. "That was seven years after he died and four hundred years ago this year," he added before going on to say, "There are about two hundred and thirty five of them remaining in the world, but ours is the only public library in the UK that owns a copy. It's extraordinarily valuable."

The nineteen seventies City Council, it seems, would have been happy to let the Shakespeare Room, if not its contents, be destroyed as it prepared for the opening of the brutalist replacement.

Thankfully, Labour had returned to power nationally in the 1974 general election and the new environment minister, Anthony Crosland, decreed that the Shakespeare Memorial Room must be preserved.

## 2 - Birmingham Central(s)

Despite three groups of conservationists threatening a "sit-in", the room was dismantled and kept in a nearby depot. Twelve years later it was finally reassembled as part of the new School of Music complex.

And now?

It's back in the library. Or rather on the top floor of the most recent library where it is something of a magnet for visitors, as I discovered on another visit (see below).

On this pleasant early Thursday evening, however, Tom and I had turned away from the site where remains of the Victorian building that once housed it were about to be built upon. Instead we gazed briefly at the handsomely engraved frontage of Birmingham's art gallery and museum, one of the city's survivors from Victorian days.

Looked handsome. Looked clean. And those two factors are connected. "Victorian architecture wasn't pleasant in the sixties and seventies," Tom reminded me. "It was damp and dirty, having been covered in soot. Now (in the post-industrial era) they've been cleaned up and done up and they look splendid."

We turned away again and gazed at the site of Tom's first library workplace. It now seems to be an Indian restaurant that shares its smoked-glass frontage with a German eating place.

"To be honest," he confessed, "I'm a big fan of brutalist buildings and I thought the seventies library was

*Libraries of a Lifetime*

*Birmingham's latest central library, designed by Meccano*

a splendidly important piece of architecture. But it really wasn't functioning very happily as what people wanted

## 2 - Birmingham Central(s)

from public libraries. More and more students were coming in, wanting to work together."

We strolled on back to the latest new library and he went on to say, "This building was designed to be outward looking. In terms of how it functions, it's probably better than the previous one."

Made through Meccano, it would seem. No, not that kind of Meccano. It's just that Meccano was the name of the Netherlands-based architectural practice that designed it.

Their construction has since won innumerable awards. Too many to fit in to this chapter, but let's just add that it was also shortlisted for the prestigious Stirling Prize for Architecture

When I visited on another day, travelling upward and onward on lengthy escalators, the "old" library of my student days seemed so last century. Which it was, come to think of it. And come to think of it again, it was built in the century before last.

On floor four of the latest library I called in at the archive section to talk to the co-ordinator Paul Taylor who confirmed what Tom had told me – the books in the Shakespeare room today are just dressing. The collection itself is kept in a special, low-oxygen, temperature and humidity-controlled environment.

"You can look at the real material with a member of staff in the room next door," Paul assured me before going

*Libraries of a Lifetime*

on to add that some of it was out on tour. "There's a project called *Everything to Everybody* and the aim is to make as much as possible available to as many people as possible. It goes to different libraries and community centres, mainly at weekends. Last weekend it was in Smethwick."

So basically what you have upstairs on the ninth floor is a very ornate room?

"Yes."

And that's for security reasons?

"Yes."

Do you get people from the Royal Shakespeare Company coming over here?

"We do. And we also get international researchers. They're primarily academics who want to see particular editions that can only be found here. The majority come from the USA and Japan where Shakespeare is quite a big thing."

## *2 - Birmingham Central(s)*

When I finally took the lift up the final five floors, it was crammed full of German students. And there were quite a few young people when we finally reached our esteemed destination. Most were taking photos with their phones of the elaborate carvings that rise majestically from floor to ornate ceiling.

Plenty of information framed on the ground floor, mind you.

It was strangely uplifting to be back in a room that had survived so many changes of location. Yet the collection that it had been built to harbour had outgrown its surroundings as long ago as 1906

That was six years before my Dad was born. He grew up not too far from here, a library with a Shakespearean connection that he would have loved.

And come to think of it, would have remembered it well when it was housed in the library before the library before last.

*The decorative ceiling and shelves of the Shakespeare Library*

*Chapter Three*

## *Whitechapel Library, Aldgate East*

And so to London and what was once Whitechapel Library, Aldgate East.

Perhaps I should put that address in quotation marks. It is, after all, the title and regularly repeated line of author, playwright and poet Bernard Kops's evocative tribute to what was once his local library. That would have been in the 1930s when Kops was part of one of many Jewish families living nearby.

*Ornate frontage rising above the grime from never-ending traffic*

*Libraries of a Lifetime*

Whitechapel Library was also, very briefly, my "local" in the early 1970s when I moved to London to work on the magazine mentioned in chapter one. It was based in Soho Square in the West End. But after work I would, eventually, head back "aht East" to the Mile End Road. I was sleeping in the spare room and sometimes on the floor of a top-floor flat next door to what was then Charington's Brewery.

Not quite posh enough to be called an "apartment", the flat was rented by Pat – Patrick Freestone, that is, a friend from recent university days – for sixteen shillings (80p) a week.

*Station next to the former library that once offered another way out of the East End*

## 3 - *Whitechapel Library, Aldgate East*

Whitechapel Library was a fair old walk down a very busy road. Can't pretend that I went there too often. Which may explain why my memories are nowhere near as vivid as those of those of Kops and many another EastEnder who grew up nearby.

Those of Jewish heritage lived in fear as the thirties wore on, for obvious reasons. But for Kops and many others this outwardly decorative building became known as "the University of the Ghetto".

It's worth cocking an ear to a bit more from that heartfelt tribute to its transformative effect on the youthful Bernard. Here's the opening verse:

"How often I went in for warmth and a doze
The newspaper room whilst my world outside froze
And I took out my sardine sandwich feast.
Whitechapel Library, Aldgate East.
And the tramps and the madman and the
chattering crone.
The smell of their farts could turn you to stone
But anywhere, anywhere was better than home."

As Kops grew older, he evidently began to understand that the building offered more than warmth and shelter. Much more. It was there that he "scoffed poetry for breakfast and novels for tea". He realised that "the door to the library was the door into me".

*Libraries of a Lifetime*

And he'd hardly be the only one. To quote from a piece in *The Guardian* written on the day of the closure by the arts and heritage correspondent Maev Kennedy, "Jacob Bronowski, scientist and historian, learned his English there and went on to become internationally famous for his television series *The Ascent of Man*. The artist Mark Gertler borrowed books on art and drew on sheets of notepaper in the reading room.

"Playwright Arnold Wesker, taken there first as a child, spurned the Beatrix Potter shelf but wept over repeated readings of *The Wind in the Willows*."

(Knowing Wesker, he was probably on the side of the weasels, the ferrets and the stoats against the lordly Toad of Toad Hall. I remember devouring his fabled trilogy of "kitchen-sink" dramas when I first came across them in the 1960s. The ongoing fight against fascism in the East End featured in one or another of them.)

Anyway, let's get back to Maev Kennedy's piece. It reminds us that Whitechapel Library bestowed on its frontage a blue plaque dedicated to Isaac Rosenberg, another local lad. And it's still there, having lasted a lot longer than the poet and painter who learnt so much from this fabled building's interior. As Kennedy points out, he "enlisted in 1914 in a regiment for those too short for general military service, and [his] body was never recovered from the mud of the Somme".

It was at the library, sometime before his dreadful death, that Rosenberg had met future artists such as Mark

## 3 - Whitechapel Library, Aldgate East

Gertler and David Bomberg. Here also that the novelists Simon Blumenfeld and Willy Goldman educated themselves.

Quite a legacy for librarians past.

*Plaque to one given life by the library before being cut brutally short by war*

\* \* \*

The library had been funded in 1892 by Liberal MP J Passmore Edwards, editor of the *Building News*. Characterised the drift away from "sermonising Gothic" towards a "warmer aesthetic combining Northern Renaissance details with Baroque asymmetry".

Apparently.

And it closed in 2005, by which time flakes of paint and plaster were regularly falling from the ceiling on to the bent heads of readers below.

Not anymore.

*The former "university of the Ghetto" still free to enter*

What was once the "University of the Ghetto" where "Lorca and Shelley said 'come to the feast'" is now part of a much-expanded Whitechapel Gallery. Two distinctive buildings side by side look very different from the outside. But inside they form an enlarged but united space for exhibitions.

Not forgetting food and refreshment.

## 3 - Whitechapel Library, Aldgate East

The first thing that caught my eye on the way in was the Modern British Dining Room and Café offering, among other things, "nutborne" tomatoes and vegan risotto with black garlic or tartlet of Portland crab with caramelised celeriac and cox apple.

Whatever happened to jellied eels? Or, indeed, sardine sandwiches.

And, more to the point, what happened to the abundance of books that entranced the likes of Bernard Kops and Arnold Wesker?

"We still have a small selection of the library's books on local studies. Some art books as well, including *The Art of the Gurkha*," I was told by my guide, archivist Andrey Lazarev. "All the books relating to the area went to the Tower Hamlets archive and they're based at Queen Mary's University. All the fiction went to the Idea Store up the road."

Quite a way up the road, as it transpired. On the lengthy trek there I found myself reflecting, not for the first time, on how the East End remained a melting pot for people with roots in very different parts of the world.

After all, Andrey had just told me that he had been a historian in Russia before moving here twelve years ago.

By that time, needless to say, the predominantly Jewish population who'd lived around the library had long since moved up north. As far north as Stamford Hill and

Golders Green in many cases. Or Hampstead in the case of Bernard Kops.

But, as Rachel Lichtenstein put it in a book of essays about Whitechapel, "It's not like a synagogue that has lost its community. It has never closed its doors."

Well, not until 2005 anyway. By that time, as Sukhdev Sandhu wrote in a piece on the closure in the *Daily Telegraph*, it had become very popular with "those from Mogadishu or Sylhet rather than the Polish shtetls. Many young Muslims, especially girls, see it as a vital breathing space away from home and the local mosque."

There are plenty of Muslim girls and women on the pavements and in the street markets en route to the Idea Store, judging by the number of niqabs and hijabs on display.

Plenty of enticing food on offer too. But my tum and taste-buds could wait a while. I'd finally reached the "Store", a strikingly modern mixture of coloured and plain glass that seemed some distance, architecturally as well as literally, from Whitechapel Library, Aldgate East.

There seem to be Ideas Stores all over the East End and beyond, offering educational courses galore. And, yes, books too.

Prominently displayed on the nearest shelf to the reception area was a copy of Monica Ali's *Brick Lane*. Well, that bustling mixture of Asian restaurants and

## 3 - *Whitechapel Library, Aldgate East*

contemporary art studios is not too far down the road from here.

One of the receptionists, Deborah Cowan, had evidently taken note of my advancing years. "People don't come in here asking for books from the 1960s anymore," she assured me before also confiding that she'd be retiring soon.

A glance at my watch reminded me that it would soon be time for me to retire from the Idea Store, head for Whitechapel tube station and quite a few stops west to meet an old friend in a very different part of London. He was going to show me a once-bustling library where he'd worked in the early seventies.

It had now been transformed into a very different venue offering the chance to "come to the feast".

*Libraries of a Lifetime*

*Chapter Four*

---

## *Westminster to Bloomsbury and Beyond*

---

Whitechapel to Westminster is a matter of nine underground stations linking two different worlds. That becomes evident once you emerge from the west-bound District Line into the packed pavements overhead and take in the view.

To the left is Westminster Bridge on which William Wordsworth once stood and proclaimed that "Earth has not anything to show more fair."

Well, it was very early on a summer's morning in 1802 and the drudgery of daily life for the lower orders had yet to commence. In the same year the same poet moaned to another poet, who'd died 128 years previously: "Milton, thou shouldst be living at this hour." If only to see, it would seem, that England had become "a fen of stagnant waters" full of "selfish men".

There are some selfish men and, indeed, women in the building across the road from the tube station. Some well- meaning ones too, doing their best to fulfil their role as MPs and civil servants.

Across another busy road from the Houses of Parliament stands Westminster Abbey. As for the "Old"

Westminster Library, as it was known even when it was still there, that stood a bit further along the road towards Victoria and a left turn down Great Smith Street.

It's now the Cinnamon Club, and the "club" is really an exclusive Indian restaurant. Considerably more exclusive than the curry houses of my youth. A glance at the à la carte menu reveals that grilled Scottish scallops with varhadi taha spices, truffle potato and Kulhapuri sauce would set you back twenty seven quid. And that's just for a starter.

Some thick hardback books and heavy tomes still line the downstairs shelves, but only for decorative purposes.

It was very different in David's day. And by David I mean David Harding, an old friend from the 1980s when we both worked on what was then the *Coventry Evening Telegraph*. In later life he would work for *The Independent* and, later still, become editor of *Railnews*. But that's another story.

He'd left school in Croydon after completing his A-levels in 1974 and, two weeks later, landed a job here in Westminster at what was then a highly regarded haven of books. "I was inspired by my history teacher who'd told me how much he'd learnt from his local library," he explained as we stood marvelling at another splendid frontage of what had once been a bustling place for borrowing and researching.

"My Dad worked at British Airways and his office was in Westminster. He was a regular borrower from the

## 4 - Westminster to Bloomsbury and Beyond

library and he got me the application form after popping in during his lunchbreak.

"We used to be very busy at lunchtime. There was a huge turnover of books," he recalled before going on to explain that the clientele was a strange mixture from either end of the social scale. "Harold Wilson was a member, as were any number of bishops and clergymen."

In answer to my obvious question David went on to say, "No, I never saw Wilson personally, but then he was re-elected as Prime Minister while I was working there so he may have been a bit busy. The Metropolitan Police commissioner Sir Robert Mark was a member too, and I did see him occasionally. Everybody used libraries back then."

At this one there were civil servants, MPs and researchers as well as pupils and teachers from Westminster School. "Then again," David went on, "there was a Church Army hostel nearby and some of the homeless chaps would come in here during the day to read the papers and get warm. The only thing was that you had to wake them up if they fell asleep."

The library also ran a book service for housebound people, apparently. And the youthful Harding was occasionally expected to go and help with that, as he well remembered. "Sometimes you'd be in rundown places and sometimes you'd be offered a sherry in rather a posh glass."

*Libraries of a Lifetime*

Well, he was eighteen at the time. And he was a "library assistant" rather than an "assistant librarian", a job for which you had to have some qualifications.

As it transpired, he also had enough A-level qualifications to study English at Nottingham University. For a while at least. "I dropped out," he confessed, "and went into journalism."

But he evidently has retained some fond memories of his six to eight months of what we might term "librarianism".

His memories of working here at the Old Westminster branch kept coming back as we slipped inside the restaurant. Of the huge wooden cabinets in the reference section. Of the balcony running round the edge of the building and the gallery above where they kept the "restricted access" books.

What did that mean?

"They were either expensive books or gynaecological books or art books and, if you wanted one, a librarian had to go and get it for you. There was a worry that otherwise those books might have things scribbled in them.

"Older books were kept in the basement and they had to be brought up on request," he confided before going on to recall that "the whole borough of Westminster had a good library service, from Victoria to St John's Wood".

## 4 - Westminster to Bloomsbury and Beyond

Back on the pavement, as a few late-lunchers savoured their digestifs, he took one last look at the building that was now supplying food for the well-off to savour rather than food for thought. Then he gave me his final thoughts on what had been his first workplace:

"The great thing was that for the price of a postcard you could order a book from anywhere in the world. You might have to wait, but it would turn up eventually.

"It was a great system and a great public service. Yet it's one of the first things that get cut when local authorities are looking for savings."

Too right and increasingly evident well beyond Westminster.

\* \* \*

Not much more than two and a half miles from Westminster stands Bloomsbury, home of the British Museum and once the British Museum LIBRARY.

The "new" British Library was commissioned to be built a mere fifty years ago to house the abundance of books that the original building was eventually incapable of housing. It finally opened its doors to the public twenty four years later, and we'll be going through those doors later in this chapter. For now, though, let's focus on the original British Library.

It had been founded in 1753 as "one general repository" for the collections of Sir Hans Sloane, Sir

Robert Cotton and Robert and Edward Harley. And as if that wasn't quite enough, the contents of George III's library were handed down to it in 1823, thus doubling the books at its disposal.

The setting for perusing those books improved considerably in 1857 when the "Round" Reading Room opened, topped by a very imposing domed roof.

Not surprisingly, perhaps, the RRR became part of London's literary landscape. George Gissing used it as the setting for his 1891 novel *New Grub Street*. "The valley of the shadow of books," was how he described it. Which sounds a little deathly. Then again, that may have been how it seemed in the silence imposed by librarians of the Victorian era.

Some of them may have experienced an attack of the vapours had they known that one of their members, Karl Marx, was using the place to work on his revolutionary notions of transforming society.

Jacob Richter was also a member some years later. And, in case you're wondering, that was a pseudonym for Vladimir Lenin. At the time he needed to cover his tracks from the Russian authorities. Not until 1917 did he himself become the ultimate Russian authority.

Other members included, at different times, Charles Dickens and Charles Darwin, George Bernard Shaw and Virginia Woolf. She used the Reading Room, apparently, as "a focal point in her examination of the exclusion of women from the literary cannon".

## 4 - Westminster to Bloomsbury and Beyond

Woolf was, however, a prominent member of the Bloomsbury Group, along with her sister the artist Vanessa Bell. Members included the economist John Maynard Keynes, the author EM Forster and the writer and critic Lytton Strachey.

Virginia and Vanessa hosted meetings at their home in Gordon Square. Discussions on matters literary and scientific may have been somewhat lively for the library, one imagines.

* * *

While we're discussing British Libraries past and present, it's time to mention Keith Railton. He has, after all, been a regular visitor to both buildings over many decades.

Still is.

No, he's not as well known nationally and internationally as the figures mentioned above. But he's "world famous round here" as a talented actor and director for well over half a century at The Criterion, our thriving local amateur theatre in Earlsdon, Coventry.

Thankfully for Keith, the current British Library is even closer to Euston Station than its predecessor. And Euston is only an hour away from the city where he has lived for most of his seventy five years.

His first seven years were spent a considerable distance from Coventry, let alone London, in Barrow-in-Furness, Cumbria. His father was a pattern-maker in the once-thriving local shipbuilding industry. A highly-skilled job, for sure.

But Railton senior wasn't sure that shipbuilding would continue to thrive as yards were already closing down. What seemed more certain at the time was that the motor industry was thriving in the West Midlands. So he sent himself to Coventry on his motorbike and secured a job, using his skills on cars rather than ships.

Then he sent for his wife and indeed his son who had, in the meantime, begun a lifelong love of books. Not at the local library – "a rather a forbidding place" – but while visiting his bed-bound grandmother with his mother.

"I used to sit my gran's bed while the grown-ups talked. Opposite was a glass cupboard full of knick-knacks and a small collection of books. One was an album of sepia pictures of my family going way back. And that sparked my lifelong interest in genealogy.

"But the main thing about Nan's cabinet was that it contained this," he added before dramatically playing some tinkling music on his phone and bending forward to lug onto his knee a copy of *Harmsworth's History of the World* before adding, "It's full of cracking stuff."

Edited by Arthur Mee, apparently. And he was also editor of *The Children's Encyclopaedia*. Both tomes were dedicated to self-education – ideal for someone like the young Railton who had a great curiosity for knowledge but was never very engaged in formal education.

## 4 - Westminster to Bloomsbury and Beyond

"Looking back at my school days," he mused, "I found that many of the subjects I was forced to learn would have no future relevance to my future life at all. Endless hours partially listening to someone trying to make me understand trigonometry, physics, algebra or technical drawing was a waste of my time and theirs.

"I was more comfortable learning the things that I wanted to learn about in the way that I was most comfortable with. That was mostly through books, and they were mostly in libraries."

*Keith the Younger*      *Keith the Older*

First came the Gulson Library in Coventry, conveniently close to the local branch of long-gone Martin's Bank where he started his career as a cashier. The Gulson had partially survived being bombed in the blitz and will feature in a later chapter.

But as Keith rose up the rungs of banking before moving into a local building society, he found himself dealing with several companies based in London.

Not surprisingly, perhaps, he used any of the free time that he had in evenings or weekends to visit libraries holding information inaccessible anywhere else. "I was always interested in British music-hall," he confided, "and, when I was trying to compile a reference book for other enthusiasts, the first port of call had to be the British Library."

Yes, that was on its original site in the British Museum. And, yes, he felt privileged to work and study in the same space as many of a famous figure who had gone before. Apart from the ones mentioned earlier, he cited Oscar Wilde, Bram Stoker, Mahatma Gandhi, Rudyard Kipling, Mark Twain and George Orwell.

"The room was as they would have remembered it," he recalled. "Mahogany and leather desks were lit by brass lamps, albeit electrified. Books were ordered through and delivered by a team of silent, courteous and efficient assistants, pushing their brass-bound trolley and handling those books with white gloves."

Times change. So does technology. But some habits don't.

"The internet is now my instant library that I can question at any time," Keith confirmed. "But it doesn't stop me still going to the British Library to look at the originals. The pleasure is still as strong as when I first went

## 4 - Westminster to Bloomsbury and Beyond

to the Gulson in Coventry, though the smell is much improved."

*\* Over half a century on from joining the Criterion Theatre (mentioned earlier), the redoubtable Railton has been a key figure in building an archive of some five hundred productions that the Coventry-based theatre has brought to the stage since its foundation in 1955. "The originals have been deposited in the city archives, held deep in the vaults of the Herbert [art gallery] as our gift to the city," he said. "There's also a selection of photographs on Coventry Digital."*

\* \* \*

Now back to London again for a guided tour of the current British Library where the first thing you see on stepping off the Euston Road is an enormous bronze statue of a naked Newton.

Isaac Newton, that is. He's bent over a pair of compass dividers while sitting on a ledge rather than standing under an apple tree. Based on a William Blake portrait, apparently, and sculpted in 1995 by Eduardo Paolazzi.

Paolazzi's work welcomes us to the expansive 'piazza'. (Why is the British Library suddenly sounding Italian?) On the other side of the piazza, the neo-gothic St Pancras Renaissance Hotel appears to be peering over the wall, its ornate towers and decorative windows a marked contrast with the library's high quality if comparatively straightforward red brick.

*Libraries of a Lifetime*

*Neo-Gothic and modernist side by side*

Architect Sir Colin St John Wilson was very much a modernist, influenced by Scandinavian design. He also had to face up to spiralling costs and government spending cuts. The lengthy process of bringing what is now a listed building into being was known as "the thirty year war".

In the real war Sir Colin had been a naval lieutenant. Which may explain the ship-like funnel jutting from the library's layered roof-space.

Never mind the roof; it was time for me to hoof it across the piazza, through the front door and see off a sandwich before the two o'clock tour.

## 4 - Westminster to Bloomsbury and Beyond

In the upper-ground floor café I just about squeezed on to the end of one of many tables lined with laptop-tappers rather than lunchers. Evidently a haven for the many students hereabouts.

There were more of them lined along the immense bookcase round the corner. The technology that makes it possible to research, write and send essays made a marked contrast with the leather-bound tomes housed in the tall, glass-fronted shelves soaring above them.

Way above, I might add. What is known as "The King's Library Tower" starts in the basement and stretches over six floors. The "King" in question was George III. As mentioned earlier in this chapter, his books were donated to the "old" British Library in the early nineteenth century and remain at the core of its modernist replacement to this day. But, as our guide Joe Filbee told us on the two o'clock tour, "Approximately thirty orders a day are brought out from there."

Only for perusing on site, it would seem. "There is absolutely no borrowing whatsoever from the British Library," Joe went on to stress. "People can order or request to see an item from the collection. We operate as an archive really. Nothing leaves the site."

Certainly not the first edition of Chaucer's *Canterbury Tales*. Nor indeed the Guttenberg Bibles, one of which was on display in the Treasures Gallery. Johannes Guttenberg was the German inventor who introduced moveable printing to Europe. His first publication came out in 1400, the year of Chaucer's death.

I've forgotten which floor our tour had reached by the time that revelation came out. But I won't forget being led into a room to cast an eye over the understandably illegible Magna Carta.

Nor, hopefully, will I forget some of the facts that Joe dropped out about this national treasure of a building:

*Just one floor of the "King's Library Tower"*

## 4 - Westminster to Bloomsbury and Beyond

How it contains some fourteen million books, which would "take you around a hundred thousand years to get through". How there are also some thirty million newspapers and magazines – everything from the *New Statesman* to the Argos Catalogue. How if they were piled one on top of the other they would reach the height of sixteen double-decker buses.

No wonder they now have to be housed at the library's additional site at Boston Spa in North Yorkshire where robotic cranes are used to retrieve specific publications from the vast pile.

Back here in London our tour found itself at one time outside a reading room packed with maps. "Four million of them," Joe reckoned, including what had been the biggest framed atlas in the world, measuring five foot nine by six foot three, from 1660 until 2012. Then the Australians came up with an even bigger one.

My head was reeling with facts and figures as I walked back up the Euston Road towards what had once been the British Museum Library.

Took a while to find the fabled former reading room, beneath that hugely impressive glass dome, where so many famous authors, philosophers, theorists and politicians had embedded themselves in borrowed books.

What's beneath the dome now?

A shop?

What does it sell?

Everything from jigsaws to jewellery, handbags to "homeware".

What Karl Marx, Vladimir Lenin, Charles Dickens and George Orwell would have made of that heaven only knows.

*Chapter Five*

# *Two Budding Brains Given Life by Yorkshire Libraries*

You may not be surprised to learn that Alan Bennett has "always been happy in libraries", although never "entirely at ease there". Despite having won no end of awards, including two Lawrence Oliviers and two Tonys, the playwright author and screenwriter has never been shy of expressing that sense of social awkwardness that is often at the core of his work.

I blame the parents.

Certainly his mother had something of a phobia about library books. "Though once a keen reader herself, particularly when she was younger, she always thought of library books as grubby with a potential for infection – not intellectual infection either," he disclosed in a lengthily reflective piece called *Baffled at a Bookcase*.

"Lurking among the municipally owned pages," he went on to explain, "might be the germs of TB or scarlet fever, so one must never be seen to peer at a library book too closely or lick your finger before turning over and still less read such a book in bed."

That article appeared in the *London Review of Books* in 2011, but many his reflections centred on Armley Library in Leeds where he spent much of his childhood and adolescence, evidently ignoring his mother's health warnings.

The library, opened in 1902, having been designed in distinctly Edwardian style by one Percy Robinson. Initially it harboured a separate "Ladies Room" and, no, that wasn't a toilet.

*Alan Bennett as he would have been in his days at Leeds Library*

Bennett best remembered the reference library which, as he wrote, "proclaimed the substance of the city with its

## 5 - Two Budding Brains Given Life by Yorkshire Libraries

solid elbow chairs and long mahogany tables, grooved along the edge to hold a pen, and in the centre of each table a massive pewter inkwell. Arched and galleried and lined from floor to ceiling with books, the reference library was grand yet unintimidating."

There were, however, "the usual quota of eccentrics that haunt any reading room that is warm and handy and has somewhere to sit down. Old men would doze for hours over a magazine taken from the rack, though if they were caught nodding off an assistant would trip over from the counter and hiss, 'No sleeping!'"

Armley Library is still open. At least it was last time I checked. As I write, you can never be certain. To quote from a revealing and thought-provoking piece by Laura Kelly in the *Big Issue*, "Since the Conservatives came to power in 2010, the austerity agenda has seen UK library numbers fall by more than seventeen per cent, from four thousand four hundred and eighty two to three thousand seven hundred and eighteen. That's seven hundred and sixty four local sources of learning and community support lost in 13 years."

\* \* \*

David Kershaw grew up in Bradford, just ten miles from Leeds, and he knows all about libraries as "sources of learning". No, he's not as well-known as Alan Bennett. But he did, briefly, cross paths with Bill Shankly and play alongside Denis Law in the junior side at Huddersfield

Town FC. Both Shankly and Law would go on to bigger things with bigger clubs. Kershaw would not.

Mind you, he did go on to become an extremely effective educationalist with many letters after his name, despite having left his own school with no qualifications whatsoever.

It was Shankly who told him that he wasn't going to make it as a professional footballer before going on to say that he really should be a teacher. He then paid for a tutor to help young David to acquire those qualifications to make it into teacher-training college.

Eventually.

But he wouldn't have made the grade(s) had it not been for Bradford's central library where he spent night after night grappling with his studies.

You can read more about that heart-warming story in David's autobiography *Thanks Shanks: how Bill Shankly bought me an education and Denis Law kicked me in the shins.*

It was ghost-written by yours truly and I was happy to return to Chateau Kershaw to listen to more memories of the "old" library in the heart of Bradford that played such a key role in his transformation from no-hoper to someone who could himself transform failing schools.

First question: was it like Armley, the library in Leeds that imprinted itself on Alan Bennett's memory?

## 5 - Two Budding Brains Given Life by Yorkshire Libraries

"Very similar. It was imposing. It was also a bit intimidating. It seemed dark in terms of the atmosphere, but there were reading lights. And when you came to sit down there was a whole reading area on a beautiful oak table. In fact, there was a huge amount of woodwork around and lights with great big globes on them."

The library was conveniently close to the Bradford branch of Marks and Spencer's where Shankly had also secured David a job lining shelves and sometimes unloading delivery vans full of fruit and veg at 6.30 in the morning.

On other days he started at seven and worked until early evening. Then he'd stroll to the nearby library harbouring a banana or a pear or a piece of "parkin". And if there's no parkin round your way that's probably because it's something of a Yorkshire speciality. A slightly gingery cake, apparently, made from oatmeal and treacle.

There were only two men on the library staff and they were expected to climb steep steps at regular intervals to replace or pluck books from the higher shelves. The other librarians were women, middle aged or elderly in appearance. And, like the book borrowers and evening studiers, they were expected to jump to at the behest of the formidable madam who was in charge.

"She was an absolute tartar," David recalled. "Used to rule the place with a rod of iron. She had a shrill voice and if anybody spoke she said, 'I'm giving you one warning.' If you did it again, she'd have you out."

*Libraries of a Lifetime*

The young Kershaw had personal experience of the eviction notice, which we'll come back to shortly. First let's hear his description of what she looked like:

"She reminded me of the headmistress from my primary school. Old-fashioned in the extreme with her hair scraped back into a great big bun at the back of her head. And she used to wear the most masculine-looking clothes."

Rather than twin-setted and pearled, it seems, she was suited and booted.

"Trouser suits weren't popular with women then, but she wore trousers. And boots. Plus a heavy-looking coat instead of a cardigan."

It seems that she also had eyes in the back of her bun. When David thought that she'd turned away, he'd sneak a nibble at his parkin or banana. Back she'd stride to proclaim that she'd told him once before that no eating was allowed. She then snatched the parkin from him and strode away.

At least he could look forward to the standard fare when he finally made it home: his mother's cold brisket warmed up with gravy and followed by rice pudding.

On one occasion it seems that he had to leave the library rather earlier than usual. "I turned round and made a sarcastic comment to someone a bit older than me about Bradford City FC. He was just beginning to reply when she stormed over and told me, 'You're going to have to go.'

## 5 - Two Budding Brains Given Life by Yorkshire Libraries

"I ignored her. Then a few minutes later I felt this heavy hand on my shoulder. 'You're going,' she proclaimed.

"I said 'for goodness sake' and she replied, 'none of that lip'. Things were getting unpleasant and I thought, oh, blimey, I can see this getting into the local paper if I resist. So I just went home two hours early, shovelled down dinner and headed for my bedroom. It was really a cramped box room, not suitable for working in.

"Downstairs we were never allowed into the front room, except on Sundays," he reminded me. "The only weekdays that I was welcomed into that hallowed sanctuary were when my tutor came to visit.

"That's why the library was valuable to me. Not just because there was more space but also because of the proximity of so many books – particularly when I was studying the British Constitution for GCE O-level. And there was also a bit of company, even if we weren't expected to talk. I didn't feel as isolated I did in the box-room.

"My parents, much as they loved me, didn't have a clue what I was doing. The tutor that came in to the front parlour was a big help, but the library gave me structure."

\* \* \*

It had opened back in 1878 and, like many another, was replaced in the 1960s by a concrete and glass structure. Sited opposite the Alhambra Theatre, it had many floors and many windows.

*Libraries of a Lifetime*

David remembers calling in in the early years of the twenty first century. By that time he had retired at the tender age of fifty nine from his role as head teacher at Coundon Court School in Coventry. Well, he had transformed it from one of the city's worst-performing comprehensives to the one regarded as the best – by the City Council, by Ofsted and by the Department of Education.

In fact, the DoE had come-a-calling on his transformative talents. They wanted him to sort out other failing schools. In Bradford, believe it or not, the city where he had been told by his own head "you're a nice lad, David, but you're not very bright".

As we now know, that long and difficult road from failure to success had begun in Bradford's "old" library. What did he think of what might have been called the "new 'un" – until 2013, that is, when asbestos in its walls and an apparent fire risk led to it being replaced by yet another new central library?

"There was much more space and it was much lighter. And warmer."

Literally as well as metaphorically, I sensed, before he went on to say that "the whole atmosphere was different".

How?

"You could talk and it felt relaxed, even though there were a lot more staff about. So it also felt comparably comfortable and welcoming. But, coming back to the old library for a moment, for me it offered a bit of security. I

## 5 - Two Budding Brains Given Life by Yorkshire Libraries

felt safe there, despite That Woman. In the end I came to look on her as a bit of a character.

"Yes, you had tramps coming in, people who were hungry and smelled a bit. But somehow the place became like a rock to me. And it gave me that sense of space."

So how does he feel about so many libraries being closed and many more facing closure?

"I feel angry. I was cabinet lead for education on Coventry City Council and libraries were part of that portfolio. Yet in 2016 I'd been told that there were plans to withdraw funding from five libraries. So I wrote a paper to present to the council called *The Golden Thread*.

"That was the beginning of the end of my time as a Labour councillor in the city where we've lived for many years. I remember being called an 'effing Tory' at one council meeting and then being told that libraries are only used by 'posh middle-class people'.

"Needless to say, I challenged that statement. I remember saying, 'Look at me. The library where I grew up was my security and my help to get on in life. You can borrow books for free and meet people. They're part of the community and part of civilised democracy.'"

Agreed. By me, that is. Not by the leaders of Coventry City Council, however. They went on to pull money out of three local libraries, including one in Earlsdon where David has lived for many years. And so have I.

*Libraries of a Lifetime*

Thankfully that decorative local treasure, built in 1912 with money provided by Andrew Carnegie, is now a thriving volunteer-run community centre offering books to borrow and buy. And more. Much more.

We'll be going in to the story behind that much-loved building shortly. But first a final word from Alan Bennett:

"In the current struggle to preserve libraries not enough stress has been laid on the library as a place not just a facility. To a child living in high flats, say, where space is at a premium and peace and quiet not easy to find, a library is a haven. But saying that, a library needs to be handy and local; it shouldn't require an expedition. Municipal authorities of all parties point to splendid new and scheduled central libraries as if this discharges them of their obligations. It doesn't. For a child a library needs to be round the corner. And if we lose local libraries it is children who will suffer."

Children and many more.

## 5 - Two Budding Brains Given Life by Yorkshire Libraries

# Thanks Shanks

### How Bill Shankly bought me an Education ... and Denis Law kicked me in the shins

David Kershaw

as told to Chris Arnot

*Libraries of a Lifetime*

*Chapter Six*

## *The Car that Crashed into the Crime Books*

The phone call came just after 7.30 on a Sunday morning. Helen Sunter had only just woken up. Somebody at the end of the line told her that the alarm had gone off at the library and, as it happened, she was first on the call-out list. "When I took the call," she recalled, "I thought it must have been a spider setting off the censors. It was that time of year."

Hallowe'en indeed: October 31, 2022.

"So I thought I'd have a coffee and a shower before I went in," Helen went on to say. "Then I got another phone call from a neighbour to tell me that there was a car embedded in the building. I rushed here to find fire engines and a police car outside. It was quite a shock."

"Here" was, and still is, Sandiacre Library in south-east Derbyshire. The car was a Mini Cooper. The driver, a thirty four-year-old man, was arrested and charged.

Despite the many road humps hereabouts he had somehow managed to travel at some speed along the road right opposite the library, round a concrete pillar and straight into the fiction shelves – "destroying my shrubbery on the way," Helen added.

*Libraries of a Lifetime*

*The Mini Cooper that did maximum damage*

Appropriately enough, the car had finally come to rest in the crime section. A police officer pointed that out to her while struggling to keep a straight face.

\* \* \*

Around this point in our conversation I asked Helen what her official title was. "Assistant in charge," she replied before adding drily, "It's like a manager but cheaper."

And my interest in Sandiacre?

Well, we lived here from 1976 to 1981. Two of our daughters were born during those years. The older one was two when we arrived and seven when we left. She would sometimes accompany me to the library on Saturday mornings and find books in the well-stocked children's section for me to read to her at bedtime.

## 6 - The Car that Crashed into the Crime Books

At the back of the building was, and still is, a park where she would play on the way and, indeed, the way back. Sometimes, when my wife needed the car, I strode across that park early on weekday mornings to catch a bus into nearby Nottingham where I was first a feature writer on the *Evening Post*, then assistant editor and columnist on the *Nottingham News* and finally a producer on BBC Radio Nottingham.

Turbulent times. But I've long retained an affection for the city and we'll be visiting its central-libraries past and present in the next chapter.

For now, though, back to the Sandiacre branch, opened in 1975, crashed into and closed in 2022. Only temporarily, mind you.

"We managed to get the place reopened six weeks after the crash," Helen recalled. She also remembered working with colleagues to clear up the mess once the car had finally been disentangled. "It was so dusty and dirty."

Rather shady too, in that part of the building that briefly became an indoor car park. As we stood there surrounded by book trolleys rather than shelves, my helpful and friendly guide assured me that a new wall would soon be on the way. With windows to let in the light, what's more.

There was no shortage of light elsewhere in the building. No shortage of laughter either from the reference section. The ladies gathered round the table for one of their regular book-club meeting were evidently enjoying their discussion of *The Authenticity Project* by Clare Pooley – a "feel-good novel", apparently, and a *New York Times* best-seller.

"We host several book groups," said Helen. "It's mainly ladies who come along but the crime-books group has quite a lot of men in it."

*Helen Sunter, the mainstay of Sandiacre Library*

\* \* \*

## 6 - The Car that Crashed into the Crime Books

At this point I noticed a large lump of wood parked on top of one of the reference bookshelves.

"Mediaeval oak," my library guide explained. "It came from a tithe barn that stood next to the church until it was taken down because it needed preserving. The local council didn't have the money to spend on that preservation so it was passed on to Bosworth Field in Leicestershire where it is now the refreshment place. That's our one remaining piece," Helen added, pointing to the log on the bookshelves.

Bosworth Field was immortalised by Shakespeare as the place where Henry VII became the first of the Tudors after seeing off Richard III. "A horse, a horse, my kingdom for a horse," were almost Richard's last words. In the play at least.

By now my memories were flowing. There was a horse in one of the open fields of Stoney Clouds, just up the road from where we lived in Sandiacre, and I used to lift up my daughters to stroke its head as it leaned over the fence.

The youngest of those daughters, now in her forties, moved back to the west side of Nottingham not long after leaving university in Salford. She now lives not far from here in Beeston with her husband and two teenage children.

One of them is an avid reader of books, bless her, many of them borrowed from Beeston Library. Still open. Still offering vital community services. So is Sandiacre's,

*Libraries of a Lifetime*

despite the disruption caused by that intrusive Mini Cooper.

*Some differing offers from the same notice board*

Time to say goodbye and many thanks to helpful Helen before heading for Beeston Station and catching a train to town.

*Chapter Seven*

# *Nottingham Central(s)*

There she was, *Lady Chatterley*, standing proud. So was her lover, needless to say. In hardback rather than in Penguin paperback, what's more, and right in the middle of just one of the shelves given over to the works of Nottinghamshire-born novelist DH Lawrence.

As those of us of a certain age may recall, Penguin had to fight for the right to publish that notorious work with its graphic sex scenes and language considered obscene. The court case caused a sensation back in 1960 when I would have been eleven going on twelve.

Like the mates with whom I cycled to school, I was already curious about sex. So we parked our bikes outside a newsagent with bookshelves and nudgingly perused what we called the "dirty pages".

No, none of us could afford to buy it. And our parents would have gone berserk had we done so. Nearly sixty five years on and nobody batted an eyelid over that once-banned book being on display here in Nottingham's latest central library.

We'll be returning to this lengthy and well-lit example of twenty-first century architecture shortly. But first a quick whip around its predecessors:

*Libraries of a Lifetime*

The first public lending library in the middle of Nottingham was housed in a narrow but decorative building in Thurland Street. It was an elaborate Gothic design of gables, arches and pinnacles that now has a nail bar beneath it and a "Custom Tattoos" sign half way up its elegant frontage.

Back in April, 1868, around ten thousand books had somehow been wedged in there before the mayor of the day, one John Barber, performed the library's official opening ceremony. Some four hundred members signed up on the first day.

Up until then it had been the "Artizans' Library". There was also a Mechanics' Institute Library, as Beeston-based author and former Nottingham University academic John Lucas reminded me. He also had a personal memory of the building that had been founded on Forman Street before moving to North Sherwood Street.

"Much of its collection was given over to popular fiction," he recalled, "but there were also shelves devoted to local labour history. If and when I didn't feel like going down to London's Marx Memorial Library for the purpose of my own research into the murky by-ways of nineteenth-century history, I could often find what I was looking for in Nottingham.

"I also found that there were men and women of formidable learning, at least some of it gained from membership of the library. First among equals of these was a wondrous couple called, believe it or not, Victoria

## 7 - Nottingham Central(s)

and Albert. They revered books, read widely and deserve to be celebrated in in any history of Nottingham libraries.

"Albert was a carpenter by trade and, after 1945, the couple emigrated to Canada, hoping for them and their two young sons a better future than stuffy, smug, class-bound England could provide. But they were soon back. Why? Not enough art galleries, not enough music and, above all, too few libraries."

Not surprisingly, perhaps, the Thurland Street premises eventually proved to be lacking the capacity to remain a growing city's central library. A new building was erected accordingly on Sherwood Street, next to what was then the University College.

It opened in 1879 and was extended in 1932 when a new reading hall was added. Plus a gymnasium, if you please. That was for the staff only and was a feature unique to Nottingham. The city must have had the fittest librarians in the land.

In 1964, not too long after the *Lady Chatterley* controversy, the city's chief librarian, one FC Tighe, caused another controversy by banning *The Adventures of Noddy*. Not because the author, one Enid Blyton, had included anything naughty in the sexual sense. No, it was because Tighe apparently felt that she didn't use a sufficiently demanding vocabulary. Nearly all her other works were expelled as well.

Heaven knows what Mr T would have made of *Lady C*. All I do know is that he was hardly the only librarian to evict Enid B from the children's shelves. The banning of Blyton went on in libraries up and down the land – much to the annoyance and sometimes the despair of boys and girls everywhere.

*  *  *

Although we had moved to Nottingham in late 1972, my memories of the Sherwood Street premises are vague to the point of non-existence. That may be because I used libraries local to our houses for the most part – first in Arnold to the north of the city and then Sandiacre to the west (see previous chapter).

The central library moved to yet another location, Angel Row, in 1977. This time the books were crammed into a building dating back to the late 1890s that had been a furniture shop and warehouse for many years.

Now that central branch I do remember, not least because of its close proximity to what was then the ABC cinema. You could return a book and stroll a hundred yards or so up the road to get a ticket for *Saturday Night Fever* or *All the President's Men*.

Last time I looked the cinema had been replaced by a coffee bar with a branch of the Premier Inn hotel chain next door.

What is now the "old" library was locked and barred with an outdated sign in the front window telling would-be borrowers that it would remain closed "until we open the new library in the Broad Marsh area development".

## 7 - Nottingham Central(s)

That sign may well have gone up in 2020 at the start of the pandemic. The latest library opened in late November, 2023. Admittedly the Covid-19 lockdown lasted for the best part of a year. But the residents of Nottingham had remained without central branch for almost three years.

In the meantime, an extremely large collection of council-owned books had to be stored in an out-of-town warehouse at a cost of well over two hundred thousand pounds.

*What is now the "old" central library*

\* \* \*

On my way back towards the recently opened twenty-first-century library, I passed the discreetly decorative frontage of a narrow building seemingly squeezed between a sports shop and a charity shop further down Angel Row.

The Bromley House Library opens out inside into a Grade-II listed Georgian building, dating back to 1816 and quite capable of housing many thousands of books. With a garden beyond, apparently, where members can browse amid aromatic plants and stone walls in the middle of a bustling city centre.

Adult membership costs a hundred and twenty pounds a year. Less than half that, mind you, for "young adults" aged eighteen to twenty five. A fine facility, no doubt, for local residents who can afford it. But this book is about free public libraries past and present.

Time to head back towards the station and, on the way, call in once more at the city's latest central library.

No sooner had it finally come into being than Nottingham City Council declared itself bankrupt. That may well have changed by the time you read this. And indeed the premises on Angel Row may well have been sold to help pay for its successor.

At the time of writing, however, all I can say is that the latest library has a sense of space and openness that its predecessors had lacked.

## 7 - Nottingham Central(s)

*The latest central library*

\* \* \*

Once inside and up the steps, the bookshelves along and across the room seemed to stretch into the middle distance. Students on their laptops were lined along large windows that spilled light right across the ground floor.

A few more students were helping to clear up after the "Messy Play" session for children. "There's sand and flour all over the floor," one of them pointed out with a shrug and a grin. Wildly excited kids were still running around, seemingly relishing the opportunity to enjoy themselves.

*Libraries of a Lifetime*

Still to come were courses on dinosaurs and Lego building that may be a little more restrained and require concentration as well as enjoyment.

An impressive selection of children's books were spread along one long wall leading to the stairs which, in turn, led to the fiction shelves along another lengthy wall. Up here and downstairs were the works of well-known poets and authors with local connections. They included Lord Byron, who owned an impressive Nottinghamshire abbey and estate. Also the less-than-lordly Alan Sillitoe who grew up in an inner-city terrace. Yes, *Saturday Night and Sunday Morning* was on show, plus many another novel and short story.

DH Lawrence had shelf after shelf displaying his works, both here and downstairs. As mentioned earlier, *Lady C* was amongst them, albeit dwarfed in size by what appeared to be an enormous copy of *The Rainbow*. Until, that, is, I realised there were two CDs inside an audio version of that complex work.

At right-angles to the first-floor fiction works were many more shelves harbouring Crime and Thrillers, Science Fiction, "Dyslexic Friendly" books. And that was just some of the specialties.

Upstairs on the second floor were works of non-fiction. Not to mention maps, musical scores, world languages and rooms to hire for business meetings.

Back on the ground floor the coffee bar was full of happily chatting women and men of all ages. And, nearby,

## 7 - Nottingham Central(s)

men and women of mainly mature years were reading papers and doing crosswords on padded sofas with colourful cushions.

To their left was a glass-fronted display of impressively carved wooden aircraft by one Ronald Ellis, born in Jamaica in 1952. He moved to Nottingham in 1986, where he apparently made his name as 'The Aeroplane Man'. He's continued to carve and his more recent works have included Formula One cars. Apparently.

*Shelves stretching into the middle distance*

*Libraries of a Lifetime*

\* \* \*

Back outside and the demolition of the Broadmarsh Shopping Centre had halted. That may well have changed by the time you read this. But for now at least the bankruptcy of the local authority appeared to have put plans to replace it with a more appealing gateway to the city centre on hold. Still, I reflected with a glance back at the building I'd just left, Nottingham at last has a library capable of displaying properly the multitude of books that it has accumulated over three centuries. And they are available to people of all ages, all classes and all races from all over this sizeable city.

*Chapter Eight*

## *From Locarno to Library*

J B Priestley's English Journey brought him to Coventry some time in 1933. He stood on corner of Cuckoo Lane and Bayley Lane, took in the view and seemed impressed how "genuinely old and picturesque" it was before going on to proclaim:

> *"You peep round a corner and see half-timbered and gabled houses that would do for the second half of the Meistersinger. In fact, you could stage the Meistersinger – or film it – in Coventry ... I was surprised to find how much of the past, in soaring stone and carved wood, still remained in the city."*

And still do, to this day. Well, in this part of town anyway. Yes, Coventry was heavily blitzed in November, 1940, and again in April, 1941. Yes, much of the city centre was rebuilt in modernist rather than mediaeval style. And, yes, the nearby "old" cathedral's interior was ruined by bombs. But its spire and outer walls still stand, one of them across the cobbles from the splendid St Mary's Guildhall, harbouring over seven hundred years of history.

Look the other way, to the far end of Cuckoo Lane, and you can see some of the few surviving Georgian buildings in Coventry. One of them was the home of John Gulson,

*Libraries of a Lifetime*

silk-broker, banker and social reformer. And library founder, I should add.

Well, he provided the land just along the cobbles on which to build a brand new public library in 1873. He also made available significant funds to stock it.

The site of what became known as the Gulson Library had once housed the old city gaol. "It was basically falling to pieces and had to be rebuilt elsewhere," local historian, author and good friend Peter Walters pointed out before pointing at the spot where one Mary Ball had been executed in 1849 in front of a crowd of many thousands as punishment for poisoning her husband.

"It was the last public execution in the city," Pete added after gesturing towards what had been the court house next door. The dock in which Mary and many another had stood awaiting their sentence still stands, albeit inside a hostelry that is now part of the Slug and Lettuce pub chain. A few yards away from the dock stands the bar above which glows a pink neon sign emblazoned with the words "Hello Gorgeous".

As for the library that once stood between the courthouse and the side of Holy Trinity Church, that's now the Turtle Bay Caribbean Restaurant. A sign outside in early November offered the chance to "Party in Paradise This Christmas".

As a Quaker by religion, John Gulson would have had a rather different idea of paradise. His former home stands just beyond the rear end of Holy Trinity. As a plaque on

## 8 - From Locarno to Library

the house's frontage points out, Gulson lived here almost seventy years, from 1835 until his death in 1904.

Eighteen years after he passed away, one of the great poets of the twentieth century was born in the same city. And another eighteen years after that, Philip Larkin left for Oxford just in time to miss the Blitz. During his childhood and adolescence, young Philip had borrowed many a book from "the Gulson". And, once he looked old enough to be served, he would lug the latest borrowings to the nearby Golden Cross. There he browsed, apparently, while glancing up at regular intervals to take longing looks at the barmaid.

The seventeenth-century hostelry has been through many manifestations internally since Larkin left, but at least its handsome half-timbered exterior survived the intense bombing of the early nineteen forties. So did the library. Well, enough of it to reopen. Eventually.

"This end of the building was largely destroyed. So were a lot of books," Pete reminded me as we strolled towards Broadgate, the city's main square. "The reference books had to be moved to what was then Mandela House. It's since been knocked down to make way for an extension to the Herbert [museum and art gallery]."

What remained of the Gulson stayed open until 1986 when the "new" library slid apart its glass doors to welcome book borrowers to what had been the Locarno Ballroom (and later Tiffany's). Of that more later.

For now, though, it's worth reflecting on Pete's comments on the legacy of another great literary figure who had lived in the city during her adolescence and early adulthood:

"The Gulson had housed the George Eliot collection. Yes, her piano is now on show at the Herbert [art gallery]. But when the City Council decided to take down the Gulson, they gave most of her legacy to Nuneaton Library."

Well, she had been born in that borough and spent her childhood there. Then again, not many cities would have given away such a priceless set of leather-bound tomes and personal artefacts.

"Typical of Coventry," the local historian added wryly. "Give away your heritage. Who cares?"

*The view that impressed JB Priestley in 1933 is still there, more or less*

## 8 - From Locarno to Library

*The Golden Cross where Philip Larkin lugged books borrowed from the Gulson Library.*

*The house where John Gulson lived for almost seventy years*

*Libraries of a Lifetime*

*   *   *

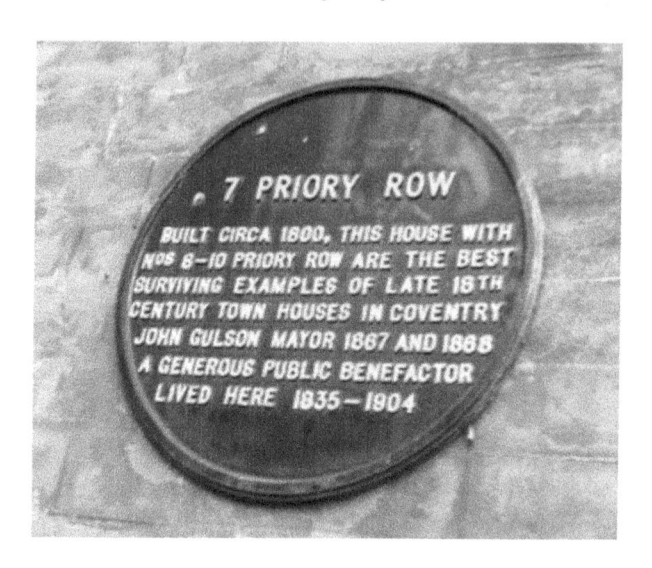

One of the other blitz survivors was Martin's Bank, which was later swallowed up by Barclay's. The Coventry central branch of Martin's was conveniently close to the Gulson for a young clerk who had left grammar school at the tender age of seventeen.

"I used to go down to the library at lunchtimes or after work," recalled Keith Railton.

Yes, him again. (See chapter four with his evocative memories of the British Library, past and present.) Sorry to interrupt, Keith. You were saying ...

"By that time I was into theatre so I was keen to look at the literary collections in the Gulson. Apart from

## 8 - From Locarno to Library

Shakespeare, there were a lot of classics, including Shaw and Ibsen, as well as some more recent authors.

"When you went in the front door, you turned right and went up a set of spiral stone stairs to a balcony that overlooked the main library. And within the balcony was an alcove where the shelves were lined with literary gems. There was what they used to call a 'smoker's chair' in bow-shaped mahogany with arm-rests. You could sit there and read undisturbed for ages."

But not smoke, it would seem. You could, however, look up occasionally from whatever you were reading and peer down to the ground floor.

"There were big tables with lots of chairs in the reference library section," Keith went on. "Also there were what looked like lecterns with newspapers chained on in case anyone wanted to nick them.

"It was always busy down there but sometimes even busier than usual, depending on the temperature and the rain. If it was wet outside, it would become even fuller than it was before. And if it was cold, people would be sitting on the radiators.

"As I was just getting into theatre, it was good to watch people. That's what actors do. They observe character, and there was such a range of characters down there. Some of them were gentlemen and ladies of the road and sometimes they masked the aroma of leather-bound books with their own particular odour.

*Libraries of a Lifetime*

"The library was an like an old Dickensian melting pot and I'll always be grateful to the Gulson for the many tips it gave me."

Helped to provide a budding thespian with the fundamentals of the stage, it would seem, both in words and in movement. Those of us who have been lucky enough to see Keith acting or appreciate his off-stage direction should also, perhaps, be grateful for the Gulson.

\* \* \*

Now, however, it's time to move on from the old to the "new" central library. Well, comparatively new insofar as it opened its doors to book-borrowers rather than band-boppers a mere thirty seven years ago, as I write.

It's only a short walk from the site of the Gulson to its 1986 replacement, which stands just down Smithford Way from the extensive side windows of Waterstone's book shop. Between the two is the comparatively narrow entrance to hmv – or His Master's Voice, as the company was known in the early days of gramophone records.

Appropriately enough, perhaps, there are still rows of vinyl LPs for sale in here, including some by local legends The Specials and one or two by Chuck Berry.

Both played a part in the history of the library building next door back in the days when it was a music venue known as the Locarno and, later, Tiffany's. In a moment we're going to hear from someone who was there in 1972

## 8 - From Locarno to Library

when Chuck recorded his UK number one hit *My Ding-a-Ling* at the Locarno on his UK tour.

*Locarno turned library*

But first let's hear again from Peter "Mr Coventry" Walters on the musical history of the building that has harboured an abundance of books for nigh-on forty years but once played host to some of the biggest names in popular music:

"Designed by the City Architects department and operated by the Mecca Leisure group, the Locarno opened in August, 1960, as a ballroom. Two years later it was hosting regional heats of *Come Dancing* for the BBC."

*Libraries of a Lifetime*

[That was long before the days when you came dancing "Strictly", I should add before apologising for interrupting again.]

As Pete was saying, "Live music began with the likes of Kenny Ball and his Jazzmen and Shane Fenton. But by the late nineteen sixties it was hosting some of the biggest names in pop, The Who, The Small Faces and Ike and Tina Turner among them.

"In the early 1970s bands like Pink Floyd, Led Zeppelin and Slade all played there, among many others.

"Radio One celebrity DJs were regular visitors, while Coventry's own Pete Waterman laid the foundations of his career in music by spinning discs at the Locarno."

Waterman would go on to become an OBE after first becoming a successful record producer and song-writer. Oh yes, and he was also, briefly, manager of local legends The Specials. Their song *Friday Night and Saturday Morning*, Pete Walters reckons, was thought to refer to the venue that had once housed Chuck Berry's 1972 recording of *My Ding-a-Ling* that I briefly mentioned earlier.

For the fuller story of that memorable evening let's hear from another former journalistic colleague of mine, Steve Evans, who was there at the Locarno over fifty years ago when he was a mere twenty-three-year-old:

"Chuck came on stage and gave us all instructions about the chorus line that he was about to sing. The girls were asked to sing one part and we chaps had to

## 8 - From Locarno to Library

contribute the other part. Not that we were told that it was being recorded. We all merrily indulged in the participation.

"Chuck made us chuckle and hundreds of Coventry and Warwickshire pensioners can now look back and claim they were once upon a time the backing singers on a track destined to reach number one. And we're still waiting for the royalties," he added before taking his tongue out of his cheek to reflect, "When I look back, it's strangely ironic that our boisterous bellowing that night took place in a building that's now a hush-hush sanctuary of silence."

Not quite as silent as libraries of old but much quieter for sure than it was the in the nights when The Who and many another rock band were playing there. The Locarno-turned-Tiffany's closed its doors in 1981, the year when The Specials recorded *Ghost Town* and many a Coventry business was also closing its doors.

At least, as Pete mentioned earlier, the one-time Locarno-turned-Tiffany's reopened as the central library five years later. And what's it like in there nearly forty years on?

We're about to find out.

\* \* \*

As usual, the downstairs windows to the left of the sliding doors were covered in parts with posters advertising everything from chess sessions to book talks to "half-term music workshops".

*Libraries of a Lifetime*

I'd forgotten that it was half-term. It meant that the place was not quite the "hush-hush sanctuary of silence" that Steve Evans had suggested a few paragraphs ago.

Once I'd scaled the two flights of stairs leading to the library, the extensive Children's Centre was full of chattering children. Not chattering too loudly, mind you. Some were reading. Some were colouring or painting. Some were concentrating hard on building models.

Quite a number of the mothers with them were wearing niqabs or hijabs. Well, Coventry is a multi-cultural city, as a sign at the bottom of the stairs had spelled out with the word "welcome" in many different languages.

\* \* \*

On the far side of the room from the Children's Centre and the Teen Zone, a quartet of venerable Sikhs sat around a table discussing matters and, in one case, perusing a broadsheet newspaper. "Helps to pass the time," he told me.

On a sofa behind him a white man was passing the time fast asleep with his arms firmly folded. At least he was sitting rather than lying with his boots on the upholstery.

Nearby were two closed glass doors, one harbouring the Virtual Reality Section, the other a Multi-Faith Contemplation Room.

## 8 - From Locarno to Library

Laptops galore were being tapped on tables around us and on the balcony above where youths and young men would once have leaned over while ogling the women dancing below.

Coventry now has two thriving universities within its boundaries and many student properties in and around the city centre. So the library is very much a sanctuary of comparative silence where they can get on with their research and writing.

One of many signs around the walls carried the slogan "Believe in your shelf". And there were books in abundance spread along and around a great splay of shelves. Those shelves were broken up every now and then by padded stools where browsers could sit down for a longer read.

*Libraries of a Lifetime*

Lengthy fiction sections were also broken up here and there by collections labelled "Poetry and Plays" or "American Literature". The latter just happened to be opposite the cricket section of the many sports books. None of my three cricket books on there, mind you. Out on loan, perhaps? Or perhaps not.

On the shelves devoted to radio programmes, mind you, I did see a copy of *The Archers Archives*, which I co-wrote with one of the script-writers. Appropriately enough, it was right next door to *Desert Island Discs: 70 years of castaways*.

Jeremy Vine's biography was nearby, entitled *What I Learnt*. From the *Coventry Evening Telegraph*, perhaps? Well, that's where the celebrated broadcaster started his journalistic career back in the 1980s when he was a young reporter, Steve Evans was a stylish writer on cricket and rugby, Peter Walters was a talented feature writer and I was features editor and columnist.

Memories, memories.

The building that housed what was then a proper newspaper is now a hotel and restaurant with quite a few of its original characteristics restored and incorporated.

I glanced down the precinct towards it when I finally stepped out of Coventry's much-valued central library. I also glanced up to see that it was open on weekdays from nine am to seven pm. Quite a few hours at weekends as well. That's considerably longer than Birmingham's

## 8 - From Locarno to Library

equivalent, which doesn't open until 11 am and is closed all day on Sundays.

Anyway, let's hope Coventry's opening hours continue.

You never know.

John Gulson would never have known that the central library he founded would be partially destroyed by German bombs and would, eventually, become the site of a Caribbean restaurant offering the chance to "party in paradise this Christmas".

Times change. But the value of libraries never does.

*Libraries of a Lifetime*

*Chapter Nine*

---

# *My Beloved "Local"*

---

The sliding doors parted company to let me through and the first thing I heard was my wife singing. So were many mothers ranged around a room lined with shelves full of children's books. Those books remained largely untouched on this, a Thursday morning.

Well, 'Rhymetime' was underway so most of the kids present were singing along with their mums, carers and one or two grandads. The only ones not singing were those with dummies between their lips.

*The Earlsdon Carnegie Community Library*

*Libraries of a Lifetime*

Quite a crowd, as I could see by peering through the glass panelled windows to the right of the desk separating book borrowers and buyers from some of the volunteers who've been running Earlsdon Carnegie Community Library since Coventry City Council planned to close this and two other branches. .

Jackie, my aforesaid wife, is one of the volunteers. And, in case you're wondering, the song wafting from the children's section was *If you're Happy and You Know it Clap your Hands*.

Almost everybody was clapping as well as singing, even those wedged on to small children's chairs. Pushchairs and prams were crammed into the spaces around shelves full of more substantial books in the adjoining room – biographies on one side and the history of warfare on the other. Between them were comfortable sofas either side of a glass table smothered with leaflets and pamphlets.

At the end of one sofa sat a self-confessed newcomer to this library, seemingly absorbed in a book on *Walks in Warwickshire*. And on the other settee was a Japanese student diligently bent over her laptop. More substantial computers were being tapped on tables lining either side of this, the "Reading Room".

That's what it says on a brown sign inscribed with faded gold lettering that dangles from the high ceiling. Like much else in this and other parts of the library, there's a distinctively post-Edwardian look about the décor installed

## 9 - My Beloved "Local"

by Earlsdon's own community entrepreneur Alan Denyer working in total isolation during the lengthy lockdown caused by the pandemic.

To the left of the sofa stands a chest of antique drawers that could once have harboured expansive underwear and substantial corsets. And atop the chest is a sizeable wooden wireless that would have transmitted JB Priestley's wartime broadcasts and the Billy Cotton Band Show.

*A retro wireless in the library*

Nearby are a rocking chair and an ornate lamp that might once have been powered by gas. And above them all is a screen that had been pulled down only the evening before to show an engaging Spanish film with sub-titles. The library's cinema club meets every month and, if the bar isn't open, you can bring a bottle or can and sip beer or wine while watching.

## *Libraries of a Lifetime*

Yes, I'd been there for the previous evening's showing. Now, with the screen rolled up, I could see the framed story of one Paddy Riordan returning to the library a book borrowed by his late grandfather, Captain William Humphries, on October 11, 1938. It was four thousand three hundred and eighty five weeks late.

Paddy had seemed happy to shell out a fine of eighteen pounds and twenty seven pence. And yes that amounted to four thousand three hundred and eighty five pennies in the "old money" – a penny for every week, in other words. That would have been the fine at the time the book had been borrowed.

The captain wasn't the only long-term borrower from the Earlsdon branch. Another book taken out not too long before the outbreak of World War Two was never returned. It was found in the possessions of one Philip Larkin when he died in 1985.

Yes, that Philip Larkin, once senior librarian at Hull University, who just happened to be one of the great poets of the twentieth century. He also happened to have been born in Coventry in 1922.

As a teenager, he used to cycle from his parents' home near the central station to visit his chum Jim Sutton who lived in Earlsdon.

On the way he would sometimes stop at this library to borrow books which he usually returned. The exception was *The Senior Commoner* by Julian Hall.

## 9 - My Beloved "Local"

Mind you, it seems unlikely that too many Earlsdoners would have been queueing up to get their hands on it. According to a piece that Larkin wrote for *The Spectator* three years before his death, it had a huge structure of tiny episodes designed to portray a complex institution at all levels. He was apparently attracted by its "brittle plangency of style and its studied circumstantial irrelevancy".

\* \* \*

As the rhyme-time session drew to a close and toddlers were being put back in their pushchairs, I made room on the sofa and headed towards the more prodigiously shelved room next door. On the way I paused to look at the table lined with jars of tea and coffee, including decaf. Not forgetting squash, apple and black currant as well as apple. Cartons of porridge were available as well as chicken and mushroom pot noodles. There was even a tin of biscuits. Not forgetting a rather different tin with a slit in the top.

Yes, you could help yourself to the items above but a contribution would be appreciated. "After all, we need to make at least a thousand pounds a month to keep this place open," I'd been told by chair of the volunteers Julie Rubidge.

*Libraries of a Lifetime*

*Julie Rubidge*

We'll be hearing more from Julie later in this chapter. But for now I continued my stroll from the sofa, past a three-tiered metal basket bulging with contributions for the local food bank. Beyond were lines of shelves offering books on an extensive range of subjects.

The fiction section extends along one lengthy wall. Nearby shelves are labelled Crime Thrillers, Cookery, Home and DIY, Foreign Languages, Horror Fantasy, Talking Books, Large print Fiction. And more.

In the Politics, Law and Social Issues section I found a book called *Britain's Lost Breweries and Beers* by some bloke called Chris Arnot. On the Classic Fiction shelves were works by rather more eminent authors, including Charlotte Bronte, George Eliot and Thomas Hardy.

At the far end of these many lines of enlightenment is a table that today was hosting the "knitter and natter"

## 9 - My Beloved "Local"

group. The ladies present were ... well, knitting and nattering beneath the high windows that run right around this splendid haven of hospitality.

Through those high windows you could see the side of Earlsdon Primary School, built in 1890, some twenty two years before the library. And, yes, the two buildings make a close and convenient partnership.

Quite a few pupils tend to move next door, particularly on Saturday mornings when the settees in the Reading Room are pushed back and folding tables are pushed up to accommodate Lego assembly, painting or the craft club.

In the children's section, meanwhile, on the third Saturday of every month, you can "read to Sophie". Not that she'd have much idea what you're on about. Sophie is a Tibetan terrier. A very benign one, I might add. Reassuring too, I was assured by her mistress Isabel Langdon who came to Coventry from Colombia.

So reassuring is Sophie that children find her easy to read to. The last time I called in to see her, the dog was clad in a Christmas jacket with Santa on the back. A little Asian girl was kneeling in front of her, reciting words dog-wards while her evidently adoring father looked on and another little girl sporting pink wellies waited patiently for her turn.

On my way to the other end of the library it was noticeable that the food bank was harbouring quite a few chocolate boxes mixed in with more basic sustenance. Well, it was the festive season – or "la saison festif", as I should perhaps put it, as the weekly French conversation classes had replaced the knitters and natterers at the table beyond the shelves.

Those are just two of heaven knows how many classes, clubs and societies that this aptly named "community" library provided space for. A glance through the *Library News* column in the Earlsdon *Echo* gave a flavour of what went on – everything from T'ai Chi to chess, crochet sessions to help with digital devices. Not forgetting a friendship group for people living with memory loss and free hypnotherapy sessions with professional hypnotherapist Louise Hall.

And more. Much more.

\* \* \*

There are also occasional "gigs" for which the five or ten quid a head door payment is usually well worth forking out – particularly so when Coventry's own indie-rock, blues and folk star Wes Finch tops the bill. Sometimes I look up from the "stage" to glance through one of the high windows to see the top deck of an eleven bus pulling up outside. A few of the many students on board sometimes look up from their phones and then look down on us with a mixture curiosity and envy.

As the *Library News* column makes plain, "We want everyone in Earlsdon and the wider Coventry area to access a warm and welcoming space, to connect with others, make new friends and feel part of their local community."

## 9 - My Beloved "Local"

That column was written by Lucy Winter, the only paid member of staff, who was diligently dedicated to her role organising fundraising and events. Her contract has now come to an end, alas.

*Lucy Winter*

Heaven knows, this library needs more than enough on the fundraising front. "We're one of well over eight hundred libraries throughout the country now run by the community rather than the local authority," chair of the volunteers Julie Rubidge assured me when I caught up with her again in the book-crammed office just off the reading room.

The Earlsdon branch was one of three threatened with closure by Coventry City Council back in 2017. How did she feel about that as one who lived nearby and had once been a library assistant across town in Willenhall before becoming a primary-school teacher?

"I couldn't really believe it. But then I kind of accepted at the time that that was the way it was. And a group called Earlsdon Library Friends had started to try and run it.

"Anyway, I'd retired from teaching by then so I volunteered to do half a day a week and that went on for about six months or so. We had a few meetings here and it wasn't an easy time as a volunteer because nobody knew what was happening and the council wouldn't tell you anything. It all seemed very secretive. There was a complete stand-off between councillors and the ELF."

And there was worse to come. Julie recalled being in Sainsbury's on a very wet afternoon "with a stroppy three-year-old granddaughter" when her phone rang.

"It was Abi, one of the people behind the ELF. She said, 'I didn't want you to read this on an email but we can no longer work with the council so we're pulling out.' At that point my eyes filled with tears and my daughter Lucy said 'Don't get upset, Mum. Just do something about it'."

She did, albeit under considerable pressure. All that had been bequeathed by ELF was a kettle and a tin with a twenty pence piece in. Meanwhile, the head of libraries came-a-calling with his deputy and a local councillor, and their message was hardly encouraging: "Unless you can get people in to volunteer, we'll close the library next week."

Julie duly plotted plans over a meeting with three others at the City Arms pub across the road. All remain stalwart volunteers to this day. So do many more after

## 9 - My Beloved "Local"

they called a public meeting that attracted no fewer than seventy Earlsdoners.

That was in 2018. And it was in September that year that charity status was granted. With it came the keys and a one-off transition payment of twenty thousand pounds.

"The council also gave us a forty per cent discount on books to loan," Julie confided. "Initially we were told that we couldn't issue 'our' books on 'their' system and communications were fraught. A pivotal point was inviting a council officer to every volunteer meeting so that trust could begin to build.

"They also maintain the building at the moment. But we're paying an escalating scale of funds towards the running costs. And we're still on the point of negotiating the next lease," she added with some trepidation.

* * *

One of the factors that helped in the transition from local-authority-run library to volunteer-run library was the unexpected donation of a considerable number of books. From a woman who lived in Australia.

"'Strewth," Julie. Please explain.

"It was a week before the Earlsdon Festival and this woman ran into the library on a Thursday afternoon. She'd been back in Coventry because her mum had died. She'd just done the house clearance and she was flying back to

*Libraries of a Lifetime*

Australia the very next day. She just said, 'I've got a white van full of books. Can I leave them with you?'"

She could. Most welcome.

"There turned out to be quite a few brand new ones," Julie went on. "That's when we decided to have our first ever book sale outside the library on Earlsdon Festival day."

Result: around eight hundred pounds profit. Further result: many more donated books available to borrow. Or indeed to buy as a vital source of income that helps to keep this much-valued venue open.

Julie has been a major player in that process. Not surprisingly, she was the one who was called upon to receive the Queen's Award for Voluntary Service, oherwise known as the MBE for volunteer groups, in 2022.

*The Queen's Award*

## 9 - My Beloved "Local"

So again not surprisingly, my final question to her was: why are libraries so important to you?

"I was always reading as a child and I went on to teach at primary schools where I saw the difference that libraries can make to children's chances."

Always have done, as I know only too well from personal experience (see Chapter One). Yes, my grandchildren spend a lot of time on their phones and, yes, many people now read books on-line. But you only have to see borrowers and buyers much younger than me browsing shelves inside and outside this precious building and in libraries elsewhere to realise that books still matter.

Going into one of over three hundred thriving branches of Waterstones nationwide will confirm it. And that's just the best known brand of many still-thriving bookshops from York to Hay-on-Wye to Charing Cross Road in London, Lewes in Sussex and more.

Now back to Coventry and, specifically, to Earlsdon where our local library offers books galore and so much more. Heartfelt thanks to the volunteers who've kept it open and thriving. Like me, they know that libraries can change lives for the better. Always have and always will.

As long as they can stay open.

**THREE STALWART VOLUNTEERS HAVE THEIR SAY**

*Rite Adams*

Rita Adams worked at Coventry University as a human resources manager. She's now a member of the library's management team and a trustee who does a couple of shifts a week on the front desk:

"I can't remember where I was first heard that the library was going to close, but I do remember feeling shock and concern. I feel very strongly about public libraries. The whole thing about reading and access to books is so important. And even though this is the digital age, books written on paper are easier to absorb.

## 9 - My Beloved "Local"

"I do sometimes look at books electronically, but I don't always take in what I've read that way. And I also like the physical sensation of holding a hardback or a paperback in my hand.

"Our mission when we started was just to keep the building open. But what became apparent very quickly was that a library generates very little income. It was the need to do that that that brought about community events. In that regard I could never have imagined the way it has developed and the success we've had.

"It's fantastic really. This is a great place to be involved with."

*Alan Blundy*

Alan Blundy was a lecturer in government and politics at various colleges in Coventry. He's now a library volunteer.

"As a small boy my parents regularly took me to Stoke, one of the three libraries founded by Andrew Carnegie in Coventry. So when I moved to Earlsdon at the age of twenty six, I was a regular library user and this building seemed very familiar to me.

"I was very upset at the prospect of such an important local facility being closed down. It would be denying poorer people, and children in particular, the opportunities that I had.

## 9 - My Beloved "Local"

"The council were trying to argue that Earlsdon's a very prosperous area that didn't really need library facilities like other parts of the city. Which is rubbish. There are plenty of relatively poor people living here.

"Without libraries I wouldn't have made of my life what I did. Yes, that was in the days before the internet and, yes, young people automatically go on-line for information. But plenty of children still use the library. And so do plenty of adults of all ages. We've become a very important community hub in Earlsdon.

"I have three children of my own and they now live here, there and everywhere. But they seem quite happy with their lives and this library was an important part of their growing up."

*Ann Wilson*

Ann Wilson is a former nurse whose father was in the air force. She is well travelled, having lived in various parts of this country and indeed the world. Returning from ten years in Zambia with her husband Ray, they finally settled in Earlsdon. Ann works at the library on Thursday mornings and seems happy to fill in on other shifts:

"I first volunteered because my sister Kim was still teaching English at the time when the council pulled out and she said to me, 'Ann, you must go and volunteer at the library and then, when I retire, I'll take your place.' But I had such a lovely time here that I kept coming as well as Kim.

*9 - My Beloved "Local"*

"It's a nice environment. It's warm. You can have a cup of tea or coffee and it gives you a good feeling to know that you're doing your bit to serve the community from top to bottom. Apart from Thursday mornings, I occasionally fill in when other volunteers aren't available on other days.

"The library is important as a social haven. So many groups come to make use of it, from the very young to the very old and all across the social spectrum. I really can't imagine Earlsdon without it.

"I was disgusted when the threat of closure came and I'm so pleased that it has become so successful."

*Libraries of a Lifetime*

## *Postscript*

Soon after I'd finished writing the last chapter of this book, the first chapter arrived back, laid out for publication with added pictures. It was time for a "read-through".

Not for the first time it struck me that there was a connection between the building where my lifelong love of libraries began and the one that I call in frequently at . . . let's say the latter years of my life.

That connection was Andrew Carnegie.

He was the man who financed both as well as some six hundred and sixty libraries more in the United Kingdom and Ireland. Plus considerably more than that in the United States.

Yes, he was a public benefactor "par excellence". And, no, I would never maintain that he was a saint. You don't go from growing up in poverty in a weaver's cottage in Scotland to becoming a multi-millionaire steel magnate in the United States without a ruthless streak.

What you might call those two UK Carnegie libraries at either end of my lifetime were in Northfield, Birmingham, and Earlsdon, Coventry. The first had to be rebuilt after being burnt down by the suffragettes just before the outbreak of World War One.

And the second?

Well, what was laughably called "the war to end all wars" was still two years away what is now my "local" opened.

Carnegie came-a-calling two years later, a few months before that carnage of uniformed human beings began. It was June the fourth, 1914, when he visited Coventry. Received the Honorary Freedom of the City, no less. From the Lord Mayor, if you please.

The mayor's name was Siegfried Bettman. Yes, he was of German origin and, no, he wouldn't last long in that honorary role once the war was underway. But for now he not only welcomed the books-buildings benefactor and his entourage from the 10.30 train; he also entertained them to lunch at his substantial house in exclusive Stoke Park.

In between, Carnegie managed to visit not only all three of his personally financed libraries in the city but also the then central library that had been funded by local businessman John Gulson (see chapter eight). Not forgetting nearby St Mary's Hall for the civic formalities.

No wonder he was so effusive about the city in his statement to a local reporter. "Few places make life for the masses as agreeable as Coventry," was part of his departing proclamation.

*Postscript*

Of course he could never have predicted that much of the mediaeval core of that city would be destroyed by German planes in a second world war that would break out twenty years after his death in 1919 at the age of eighty three.

Nor could he have foreseen the coming of the internet. In the circumstances he might be pleased to have known that so many of the public libraries that he founded are still open, from Dunfermline where he was born to Portsmouth on the south coast of England.

Along with many more, I might add. Be they run by local authorities or volunteers, they remain a source of information, inspiration and the instigation of social events.

And long may they stay so. Without them we are a less civilised society.

*Libraries of a Lifetime*

## *Biography*

Chris Arnot has written sixteen non-fiction books. Small Island by Little Train was published by the AA in 2017 and shortlisted for the Edward Stanford awards for travel writing the following year. Marcus Berkmann called it "very much a state-of-the-nation book" in his Daily Mail review.

Chris also wrote four of the Britain's Lost series for Aurum. Britain's Lost Cricket Grounds was reprinted twice after some glowing reviews. The late Frank Keating described it as "a coffee-table classic for and of posterity" in The Guardian and Jim Holden hailed it as "the best sports book of 2011" in the Sunday Express. Billy Elliot creator Lee Hall called Britain's Lost Mines "an extraordinary gallery of lives and landscapes".

As a national freelance journalist for a quarter of a century or so, Chris wrote for the Guardian, the Independent, the Observer, the Times and the Telegraph. And he was a regular contributor to the Sunday Telegraph's Pint to Pint column, a collection of which was published in hardback in 2016.

*Libraries of a Lifetime*